The StarPals™ Series
Presents

Haley Humble

By Kimberlee Schultz
Illustrated by Matthew Warshaw

Published in the United States

Text/Illustrations Copyright © 2011 Kimberlee Schultz and StarPals Press

The StarPals Series books are available at special discounts for bulk purchases for sale, fundraising or educational use. For details contact Special Offers at www.TheStarPals.com

Record for this book is available through the Library of Congress

ISBN 978-1-46109-110-3

Hello, my name is Haley Humble.

I love to practice being humble. It is my favorite game.

We can practice as a team with my StarCousin Erin.

Would you like to play and be my StarPal?

I am helping dear StarCousin Erin study today.

We use the StarPal flash cards to help prepare for her Math test.

Erin thanks me for helping her earn an A+ on her test.

I humbly accept her appreciation and give her a high five.

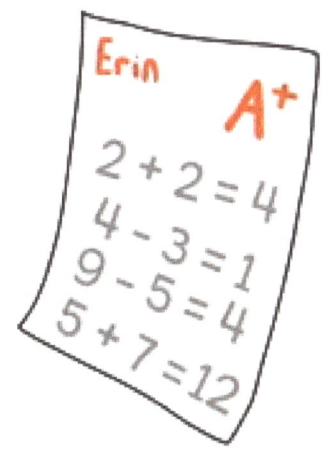

I am planting a new tree in honor of Arbor Day.

I humble myself before the Earth and thank the tree for giving us beauty and fresh air.

I entered a poster contest to help doggies find a home.

The local paper said my artwork won first place!

My heart is happy as I gently add the article to my scrapbook. DOG

StarCousin Erin and I decide to surprise Mom and we clean the dishes.

Mom is SUPER excited and thanks me!

I humbly accept Mom's praise and tell her, "It was a team effort with StarCousin Erin."

Dad says, "We have a new project."

We are going to clean the garage and get ready for our great big sale.

It's going to be fun to see what we will find!

As we sort through the boxes of stored goods, we discover many special gifts to share with other children.

We cheerfully set them aside for our annual toy drive.

As we deliver the toys to the families, we get to see the happy smiles on their faces.

The gift of surprise in their eyes fills our hearts with joy.

StarCousin Erin comes over to read my StarPals' books.

I introduce her to the seven virtues and we play The StarPals Board Game!

Treasure Chart

Fill your treasure chart with stars and celebrate your good deeds!

StarPal Name: Haley Humble

✦✦✦✦✦✦✦✦	Monday	Tuesday	Wednesday	Thursday	Friday	Saturday
Patty Patience	⭐		⭐			
Korey Kindness	⭐		⭐			
Haley Humble	⭐	⭐	⭐			
Tommy Truth		⭐				
Shari Sharing	⭐	⭐				
Tobey Thankful	⭐					
Livey Love		⭐				

Visit Us At www.thestarpals.com

Let's shoot for the stars and track our good behavior on our StarPals Treasure Chart.

Our chart helps us see our daily humble deeds and shows others our great big heart.

For special discounts on bulk shipments or to order your StarPals Treasure Chart, visit us at www.thestarpals.com

www.ingramcontent.com/pod-product-compliance
Lightning Source LLC
Chambersburg PA
CBHW060815290526
45792CB00005BB/1659